Learning from Experience

50 Principles for Leading People and Managing Programs through Trials, Tribulations, and Successes

DR. MARK P. MICHELS, LTC, USA (RET)

WESTBOW
PRESS®
A DIVISION OF THOMAS NELSON
& ZONDERVAN

WestBow Press books may be ordered through booksellers or by contacting:

WestBow Press
A Division of Thomas Nelson & Zondervan
1663 Liberty Drive
Bloomington, IN 47403
www.westbowpress.com
844-714-3454

ISBN: 978-1-6642-7496-9 (sc)
ISBN: 978-1-6642-7497-6 (hc)
ISBN: 978-1-6642-7495-2 (e)

Library of Congress Control Number: 2022914465

Print information available on the last page.

WestBow Press rev. date: 08/17/2022

Contents

Preface

This book offers fifty principles based on real-world failures and successes in leadership that I have experienced or had the privilege of witnessing in action. I accumulated much of the book's content through my thirty-year career in the US Army and more recently in my consulting business. In each section, I provide a short statement of principle and explain what it means and how to make practical use of it. Some principles are illustrated with anecdotes or real-life examples.

I hope the reader gets a clear sense of the differences between "managers" and "leaders" and how important these two roles are for taking your company or your military career to the next level. When you deal directly with people 90 percent of the time, you are leading; when you are working with schedules, product development, and other aspects of process or procedure, you are managing. If you are a manager and want to learn to be a leader, this book offers hard-earned guidance on how to overcome and excel in life.

I refer often to the "mission," a given written or verbal order or several specified tasks or accomplishments that must be completed to achieve standard requirements. You will learn to utilize and identify situations in your life—you might think of them as missions—where management or leadership techniques are required to maximize your potential, mentor others, free yourself up, and accomplish your dreams.

I want to extend a special thanks to Barry Chametzky, my long-time friend and editor. He has increased my writing skills and helped me grow as a professional communicator. Through doctoral course work to my final manuscript, he has put up with my grammar and spelling mistakes and never showed one bit of frustration. I enjoy writing now because of his mentorship and more importantly his friendship. Thank you, Barry—this first book is for you.

Dr. Mark Michels, DBA, PMP, SMAC, LSSGB, CLC
LTC, US Army (Ret.)

Dr. Mark P. Michels, LTC, USA (ret)

Leaders and Managers

Everyone can be a manager, but not everyone can be a leader.

At leadership debates, it is quite common for people to state that certain individuals are just natural-born leaders. One great leadership trait is having the cognitive ability to understand second- and third-order effects almost instantly, while others are still trying to understand direct effects. This personality trait alone does not make an effective leader. But when combined with confidence, discipline, and a sense of purpose, it makes a good one.

The ability to convince people to act is only half the story. The other half is learning to manage programs. Leaders can, in some circumstances, be limited in the scope of influence. But managers will have the skills to scale actions up and down to achieve mission requirements, while sometimes ignoring the human side of care. The military has understood the differences between leaders and managers but has never defined it within formal schooling.

We have a saying in the Army: "Mission first and people always." Not everyone is the total package, but putting managers with leaders is a win-win situation and a hard combination to beat. One key to mission success is recognizing each person's strengths and weaknesses and pairing up a leader with a manager to develop a great leadership team.

2

Let Conscience Be Your Guide

Sometimes doing the right thing means you have to listen to your conscience.

Whether we're in the military or civilian workforce, we all have norms that require discipline to maintain. No matter what the norm or standard is—showing up to work on time, wearing the correct personal protective equipment (PPE)—these standards need to be enforced. I have two examples of how listening to my conscience has served me well.

The first was when I was stationed at Fort Eustis, Virginia, and I became a certified hunter education instructor. A lot of people registered for the class and showed up, so I was pleased with the turnout.

During the class, there was a block of instruction about ethics. I always posed this question, and I always got mixed answers: if you shot a deer on your property and it jumped over a fence onto someone else's property, and you can see the expired deer only ten yards into the adjacent property, what do you do? Keep in mind, every hunter has the responsibility to make a reasonable attempt at retrieving the game animal they attempted to harvest.

In Virginia, the law does not define what is "reasonable," but there are generally accepted norms. So the two most popular answers I get are "hop over the fence and retrieve the deer" or "find the landowner and ask permission to enter their property." If you ask the landowner and they deny you access, all you can do is get law enforcement involved. The correct and legal answer is to ask permission from the landowner.

After the course was over, hunting season came only three short weeks later. About two weeks into the regular deer season, I ran into one of my students in the post gym. This gentleman was one of the people who stated he would jump the fence to retrieve the deer, to do his due diligence for the harvest. He explained to me that he had run into the exact circumstances of the ethic question I posed.

But instead of jumping the fence, he found the landowner and got permission to retrieve the deer. It worked out extremely well for him. The landowner helped get the deer with his tractor, loaded it up in his truck for him, and even gave him written permission to retrieve deer in the future. In this case, being ethical and listening to his conscience helped him for years to come, and he developed a friendship from doing the right thing.

Example number two takes place at another army post. It involved a soldier who always showed up on time, was in the right uniform, and completed the work assigned very consistently. By all standards, he was a great, dependable soldier … until he started to miss morning formations, come late, and show up as if he had never gone to bed. His work started to lack, and he became very quiet and kept to himself.

The soldier was counseled verbally and in writing to correct his behavior. But he was still getting worse. At this point, the next step was to issue an Article 15, nonjudicial punishment. Instead I decided to question him again about the reasons behind his poor behavior, and as always he gave no excuses. After I talked with other leaders, we decided to conduct a unit-wide health and welfare inspection.

For a health and welfare inspection, the command goes to your place of residence and looks inside and out, ensuring the soldier's living conditions are acceptable by military standards. The barracks were inspected first, and the following day on- and off-post housing.

During the inspection of the soldier's home, the platoon sergeant found out that his living conditions were poor and his children were being neglected. The soldier's wife was suffering from postpartum depression, and she was doing nothing to clean the house, feed the children, wash clothes, or attend to other basics of healthy family life.

Discovering his living conditions, the leadership team had his wife seek counseling, and other soldiers volunteered to help get his home in proper order while his wife was getting better. About two to three weeks later, another inspection was conducted. The platoon sergeant found the soldier's home dressed right—"dress right, dress!" being a specific military command also used in the general sense of maintaining good order and discipline. The children were wearing clean clothes, with the lawn mowed, dishes washed, and floors mopped. The soldier's wife was now going to counseling two to three times a week.

The moral is, if we as leaders had just gone along with progressive punishment, we never would have been able to help this young man's wife and make his home safe for his children. If Article 15 had been given, it would have changed nothing at home and probably would have made his situation worse.

I don't know where this soldier is in life now, but I do know he was going down a path of destruction, and leaders listening to their conscience and not just punishing this young man led to him reenlisting for another four years.

3

Learn to Listen

You're never so high in the corporate structure that you shouldn't listen to other people's ideas.

I learned this lesson quite early in my military career: if I had gone along with my ideas alone, we would have failed the mission. Effective leaders at every level—tactical, operational, and strategic—who listen to peers and subordinates alike are more likely to make educated and informed decisions. Making key and essential decisions in a vacuum when you have plenty of time to conduct planning, risk assessments, and rehearsals is a recipe for failure.

Taking the time even for a quick one-minute net call can save lives and property. A "net call" in the military is when one person talks to multiple people at the same time to disseminate information quickly. The military has recognized this relationship between leadership for a very long time, placing the commander and advisor as a team, like a company commander and first sergeant, or a brigade commander and command sergeant major. This type of relationship is the foundation of effective leadership. When leaders provide an open forum for their subordinates to speak, it encourages active engagement in their opinions and ideas.

One example that comes to mind happened while I was in the Army. I was assigned to attend a planning conference at Fort Bliss, Texas. My task was to provide insight into our organic capabilities and how they should be tested on the battlefield for data acquisition required to make future capability modifications. During planning meetings, the senior leader from each organization had a seat at the main table, and the rest of the planning team sat in a row of chairs behind the senior leader. This arrangement promoted conversations during breaks and the passing of notes when required.

This particular meeting was all about combating the effects of weapons of mass destruction in a battlefield environment. With me I had the most senior noncommissioned officer (NCO), who had the most years of experience in this type of scenario. Each capability was given an hour to present their proposed execution plan during the exercise, followed by a question-and-answer time.

During every brief, I had an uneasy feeling but couldn't quite place what was wrong. Prior to my turn to brief, my senior noncommission officer requested a ten-minute break. We went on break, and immediately, the Master Sergeant took me aside and asked if I noticed something wrong with all the briefs. I said yes, but I couldn't quite figure it out between the downwind hazard area, the level of PPE, or actions on the objective.

The Master Sergeant explained that he saw the same mistakes I did; however, he knew what the root cause was that was giving me angst, and how to fix it. We discussed the multiple problems we identified and quickly developed a pitch to the planning group that changed the entire operation.

Let's just say the planning group wasn't happy with our discovery, as they had to go back and modify their planning documents. But the exercise leaders and controllers were very impressed by the team's insight and commented on the discovery in an aside conversation. What my team discovered was the key element that the exercise control group was going to use to disrupt our entire movement plan.

If this planning were for a real-life event and I as the senior leader had not listened to my teammates, we could have killed thousands.

Don't think for one minute that you are the smartest person in the room. There is always someone who has more education and experience and can provide mentorship and counsel to make informed decisions.

4

Not Everything's an Emergency

A leader knows that not every situation requires an emergency meeting.

In the military, it is made clear what meets "wake-up requirements," as we used to call them. These events are usually written down under the title Serious Incidents or Commander's Critical Information Requirements (CCIRs). These events could entail deaths, arrests, security breaches, adverse public media, accidents, and other such consequences.

Of course, leaders always have the discretion to make a phone call—with one caveat. That caveat is "Why are you calling, and how does it affect the mission or our service members?" and it better be convincing.

However, not every event is black and white. It may require different degrees of effort in collecting facts and opinions to make a sound decision. A leader who can discern facts from opinions, and who knows and understands the difference, can prioritize efforts in so-called emergencies. Having this knowledge then allows more time for high-priority tasks and less time for something that potentially could be handled at a much lower level.

This leadership trait takes time to understand and learn. Sometimes it is just a matter of understanding what the boss wants and what type of risks they are willing to take or accept.

5

Ask Questions

The best leaders are the best listeners, so ask the right questions.

Early in my career, I thought leadership was making decisions quickly as Infantryman Michels ran around the woods with his hair on fire and decisions were made almost by the minute. It seemed that the opposing force always knew what our plans were, and we had to adjust our scheme of maneuver on the fly. Later—much later, actually—I noticed that the best decision makers were the ones who took a tactical pause and listened to whoever was presenting information or status instead of making rash decisions with minimal input.

Now that I'm retired from the military and consulting for businesses, I find myself often asked by my clients after a problem arises, "What would I do to fix this?" It always amazes me that a business owner wants an immediate solution. My response is always, "Let me talk with the people involved first, and then I will provide my recommendation."

Most of the time, after listening I've found that the people who either created the problem or witnessed it are able to solve the problem themselves. Sometimes the problem is just a misunderstanding that, when verbalized, brings to light a clear solution.

6

Ask the Right Questions

Asking the right questions is as important as making decisions.

It's important to ask the right questions, but how do you arrive at what the right questions are?

If you get a twenty-four-hour read-ahead prior to any brief, then consider yourself lucky. A "read-ahead" is a document, usually in a form of a brief or presentation, provided to the intended audience in advance of presentation time, which may not be possible when operations develop faster than briefs can be updated. And if you do get a read-ahead, you must take the time to read it and make notes, whether you are at home or en route to the meeting. It's important to read the brief twice. The first read is to ensure that the brief meets your overall intent, and the second is for writing down notes.

There are five general questions I always asked myself:

1. What types of risk does the staff identify, and how are they mitigated?
2. Are key and essential tasks being completed and on time?
3. What are the command and reporting lines of communication?
4. What does mission accomplishment look like?
5. What resources do we lack to make everything work together?

Depending on things like the type of brief (for example, a quarterly update brief, or a new equipment fielding brief), you can ask the aforementioned questions and still get topic-specific answers.

Once you have written down your notes, refrain from asking your questions until the end of the brief, as the presenter might answer some of your questions. If by some chance the person does answer every question that you had written down in advance, do not end the brief without asking at least one question or opening the floor to questions. In my experience, it is not uncommon for someone to ask a question from a different point of view that may spark a spirited debate and completely change the scheme of maneuver.

7

Making Mistakes

Don't be afraid to make mistakes now to avoid making more serious mistakes later.

Not all mistakes are created and viewed equally. For instance, forgetting to check the oil in your vehicle and blowing up your motor is a costly mistake. A more extreme example is the loss of a person's life. Nobody likes making mistakes, but peacetime is the time to make them. During the planning phase of any effort, whether taking out the garbage on an icy day or planning for a combined arms maneuver, mistakes are inevitable, and assessing lessons learned is an essential tool.

Do your research, and seek out documents and people who have had the experience of what you are trying to accomplish. Ask questions, and don't forget to seek counsel from your peers and subordinates. As you read this, you might be thinking, *Why ask your subordinates?* The answer should be clear: a leader may not be as experienced as someone who has been in the same position for a long time. This type of relationship can be proactive in mitigating or avoiding mistakes.

Throughout military history, the military has teamed up a new officer with an experienced noncommissioned officer (NCO). It is the job of the noncommissioned officer to teach and mentor the new officer even though he or she is the officer's subordinate. A good NCO can make or break an officer's career. With this relationship, the military has placed checks and balances in the command structure.

As a business consultant, I run into risk-adverse people and business owners all the time who are afraid to change or try new things. Once I demonstrate how the positive change outweighs the negative effects, it becomes much easier to execute the new plan and seek further efficiencies.

On the other hand, some business owners are ready and willing to make changes *right away*, without much or any planning. This is a recipe for guaranteed mistakes. My retort to any CEO or board of directors is this: "We can slow down and make a plan, mitigate risks, and align resources in a timely fashion, because we are not getting shot at or mortared." Nine out of ten times, this little retort puts planning efforts in perspective.

Don't get me wrong: some mistakes are bad. But if proper planning is conducted, major mistakes can be mitigated or even eliminated. Learn from the mistakes that were made, and document them in a "lesson learned" body of knowledge so that they will be remembered. Hopefully, someone will read about them later and not make the same mistakes you did.

8

Improve Thyself

Seek self-improvement through any means necessary.

We all have heard the advice to find a mentor and seek self-improvement, but what does it take to find one, and how do you know you've found the right mentor? As a person who asks for help only when I absolutely have to, I've never come right out and asked someone to mentor me. In fact, I avoided it at all costs and probably passed up plenty of smart people who could have helped me along my career. I, however, choose to be mentored through self-discovery and observation from afar.

When I was going through a required reading list for senior officers, I found that many of the authors just took credit for what is already occurring. So in addition to reading, I observe and listen to my subordinates, peers, and leaders and see how they handle situations and people. Some of the best lessons I learned in the military came when I was a private in the junior enlisted ranks, E-1 through E-4. I was platoon guide for most of basic training and got to speak to the senior drill sergeant at length. He gave me some of the best advice I ever received: show up on time and in the right uniform, and the rest will work itself out. You might think this would be common sense, but many fail at this simple task.

Next was a sergeant first class in my infantry unit named Noel E Clemens. He was my recruiter, but when I transferred back home after training, I worked at the Army recruiting station and got to return home to my family every night. SFC Clemens taught me selfless service and what it really meant. He was a bit of a jokester, but when it came time for work, he was all business. I was responsible for leads, transportation to and from the MEPS, and documentation. He showed me my left and right limits. As long as I stayed within those limits and made mission, he would stay out of my business and let me do what I wanted to do. When my plan didn't work, we followed his plan, and for some reason his plan always worked better than mine. However, he never stifled my enthusiasm for wanting to try new methods to obtain recruits to see if my methods worked. The recruiting station is where I learned the importance of an after-action review (AAR).

As a headstrong eighteen-year-old, I did AARs quite frequently, but I always walked away with at least one valuable lesson. I spent a lot of time at Fort Bragg with my first platoon sergeant, Staff Sergeant Jackson. I can picture him like it was yesterday, drinking at a bar with him as he told stories about his career as a lifelong paratrooper. SSG Jackson was quite well known, as everyone knew of his accomplishments. Most of the people who greeted him were senior NCOs and senior field-grade officers.

I once asked SSG Jackson how he knew all these people. He replied that they were in his squad, or they were his second lieutenants in charge of the platoon that he had to train. Of course, you know the next question I asked: "How come they are senior NCOs and officers, and you are an SSG?" His reply was that he worked hard and played harder and got caught. I asked if it bothered him at all. He said that he might not obtain senior NCO rank, but as long as the officers and NCOs moved on to do great and wonderful things in the military and have a great career, he had done his job.

I found this statement inspiring. He knew that he was paying for the sins of his past, but as the people whom he mentored surpassed him and went on to be great people, he felt that rank did not matter, as they all knew what SSG Jackson did for them.

Dr. Mark P. Michels, LTC, USA (ret)

I have found many people like SSG Jackson in the Army and in many joint assignments over the years. I have shown up for first formation on time and in the right uniform, and taught people how to shoot, make budgets, set up uniforms, plan theater level missions, how to march, counsel people … the list goes on. As I said at the start of this section, I never asked anyone to be my mentor. I just watched from a distance, read books, and made lots of mistakes. If you choose to find a mentor, that's up to you; what I can say is that it's a lot easier going through life with someone looking out for you, and when you get the chance return the favor someday, they might just turn out to be lifelong friends.

9

The Smartest One in the Room?

Don't be hurt or intimidated if you're not the smartest person in the room.

When you are in charge of a group of people, whether it's as a commander or as a facilitator of the Agile morning stand-up meeting,[1] don't be surprised to find that you are not the smartest person in the room. If you are reading this book, you already crossed many hurdles and discovered that maybe someone can teach you other leadership skills or hone the ones you already have. Don't get upset; just ask a lot of questions.

To start, you might be wondering what type of questions you should ask. The answer is not simple, but I'll illustrate the techniques I use to ask questions so I have a better understanding of what and how events should unfold without making myself look silly.

Also, realize there is a sniper in every planning team, so be prepared to handle that person.

There are three 100-percent legitimate questions to make people think and learn how you think. The first is risk. There are three types of risk: tactical, operational, and strategic. In every planning group, someone always has to measure risk to mission accomplishment,

---

[1] In Agile project management, the stand-up morning meeting, usually short in duration, is convened for leaders and staff to briefly discuss daily tasks and outcomes for daily or weekly deliverables.

resources, people, movement, and media. Select the best risk management plan, and ask if the planners considered others. Good planners will provide a brief explanation of risk.

The second question is, "Would you please tell me how each individual plan of action meets the guidance and intent provided?" This is a graduate-level question requiring a graduate-level thinker. As a briefer, I would always have a copy of the mission statement from higher-ups as well as ours, with the key tasks associated within reach for such a question. If I was not asked this question, I made sure it was part of my summation.

Third, ask about second- and third-order effects of the mission or plan, depending on what your team is planning. For instance, if your company is planning for a merger, one second- or third-order effect could be employee retention rates, benefits retention, and an approximate time to break even from the initial buyout. As a military example, I had the privilege of making theater-level plans to mitigate effects of weapons of mass destruction on the battlefield. Some of the residual effects of WMD are radiation, water contamination, locations of factory or containers that have toxic chemicals for manufacturing, and civilian population migration. These effects are just a few we as planners had to consider after our normal mission was completed.

If you remember just a couple of these questions, you never have to be the smartest one in the room, but you must be engaged and ask the important questions that keep everyone thinking.

10

Facilitate and Enable

Your main job as a leader is to facilitate and enable others to do their jobs.

As a leader in the military or in the corporate business realm, your job is to enable others to do theirs. That does not allow you to sit back and watch the world go by, and it does not relinquish your responsibility to provide guidance and direction. However, if you did your job and your underlings have a clear idea of your intent and vision, then you need to work on risk mitigation strategies.

A good brief will always have some sort of risk mitigation measures, so this is where you come in. For instance, envision a scenario in which your staff is planning on holding a huge outdoor event to showcase the new products your company will roll out next year. I'm sure that a part of the brief will entail a discussion regarding inclement weather and plan-B measures in case it occurs. During the brief, your staff may have stated that the tents are ordered but the delivery date has yet to be confirmed. If you, as a leader, feel that making a one-to-one phone call with the owner of the tent rental could help, it is your duty to do so or at least to offer.

The same is true for a military event. Sometimes things just magically get done when commanders talk.

Also, provide the time and resources to separate planning staff from the daily grind so they can concentrate on planning. It will pay huge dividends during the execution phase, as staff members tend to develop more feasible, acceptable, suitable, distinguishable, and complete plans when you enable their success.

Dr. Mark P. Michels, LTC, USA (ret)

11

Becoming a Leader

Leaders are not born; your social and personal environments shape and mold you.

Know yourself and seek self-improvement. If you spent time in the military, I'm sure you heard this phrase a lot. Apply it to your learning style and decision-making. When we are born, our genetics provide the building blocks for the rest of our lives. These building blocks may be beneficial to learning the basic movements and thinking to sustain your life, but as we get older, those basic thoughts and movement are altered by our mental and physical growth.

There are several stimuli that shape our learning, such as pain, euphoria, greed, or gaining a better understanding of the world around us. Motivations vary among individuals, but the one thing we all have in common is that we learn every day, and our motivation to learn varies and has different outcomes because of the environments our caregivers provide or the situations in which we place ourselves. As independent adults, we have multiple means and ways to educate ourselves in the needs, wants, and desires of learning: we can go to college, join the military, complete a job training course, read books, watch movies—the list could go on and on. The main point is that there are many places and resources available if individuals want to learn.

Learning and retaining skills and knowledge is fundamental to being a leader. For some people, learning may come easily, but

I struggled my whole life with learning. However, I found ways to improve my learning and retention in order to be a good leader.

To give an example, I'm going to take you back to my enlisted days going through Drill Sergeant School (DSS). In DSS, we had to memorize pages of script to recite to the trainees in several blocks of instruction daily. It was expected that we learn these scripts every three or four days. Some of the scripts were more than four to five pages long. And along with that work, we were still expected to complete other classes and various physical activities.

I struggled with memorization—until we started to act out what the other person was saying. So when I was reciting the script of how to render a proper hand salute, my demonstrator would do only as I instructed, and nothing more or nothing less. It was like I discovered America! I found out that I was a visual and tactile learner. I had struggled with memorization, but with the help of others as my visual aides, I passed DSS.

Knowing what kind of learner you are is only half of learning how to lead others. When you find your learning style, embrace it and seek others who learn the same way as you. They might have tricks they use to obtain and retain knowledge.

Finding people who share a similar learning style as you is just a start. Next is the hard part: placing yourself in the most positive location and making logical decisions on what you want to learn. Some people might be confused by this last sentence, but I will break it down by providing you a personal example. It's all about backwards planning and learning what the requirements are for what you want to do.

I had just turned seventeen and knew I did not want to stay in my two-traffic-light town. I wanted to experience other places and people with different ideas and cultures. I was told that college would be the best place for me to learn these things, but being from a financially conservative family, I did not want the student loan debt usually associated with college. So I considered the military.

The military offered travel, new skills, and money for college.

I did my homework by watching recruiting movies and talking to several veterans I knew. I concluded that I was going to join the Army National Guard part-time and go to college full-time. When I had all the facts presented to me, it was a very logical decision to make, and I made it in fewer than four days.

I went to basic training, and I met people from different cultures and around the world, with different religions, races, and skin colors. Later that fall, I went to my first college semester and lived in the dorms (which were a lot nicer than my Army barracks!) and again met people of different cultures, religions, races, and skin colors.

I had met my first major goal that I set for myself at seventeen. I left my little town; I was learning about our justice system in college, received training through the Army, and met wonderful friends with whom even to this day I am in contact. These goals started to shape me as the leader I wanted to be in the future.

As I progressed through the ranks in the Army, I went to every school they would send me to, and in college I would volunteer for elective projects for the extra learning benefit. The small goals I set for myself, along with identifying my learning style, set the building blocks for my military retirement as a senior field-grade officer as well as for obtaining a doctoral degree.

Play Your Part

**Looking and acting the part of a leader is just
as important as being one.**

This lesson may seem elementary in theory, but in practice you
would be surprised to know how many people make mistakes and
don't understand it.

Back in the day, Private Michels had a platoon sergeant who
took the time to meet with all of his new recruits and do verbal and
written counseling. He was a skinny, light-skinned, freckle-faced
man who walked with a limp, and a very soft-spoken man to whom
other platoon sergeants went for guidance when they had issues or
concerns. I was very fortunate to have his leadership in the early
stages of my military career.

When it came time to practice what I learned in Infantry School
in the field, he was second to none when night operations started.
For the first two or three days, he made me the radio man so I could
learn how and when to communicate to higher headquarters or to
the other members of the platoon. I was also able to watch him plan
and execute raids, insertions, and passage of lines with as few as
three sentences being spoken throughout the entire platoon. Field
craft was his forte, and it showed. I knew that his mastery of these
types of operations did not come from doing one weekend a month
but from years of active duty in the field and several deployments.
This man was wise beyond his years.

One day, I sat next to him in the chow hall and asked him how he got his limp. His reply was short and to the point: he said he got hurt in an accident in Vietnam. I didn't want to pry into more details, as I had to clean up the mess hall and get ready for a uniform inspection that afternoon. During that afternoon, he made sure our uniforms were fitting correctly and that every medal and ribbon on the uniform matched our personnel file.

As we lined up for the inspection by the company commander and first sergeant, my platoon sergeant reappeared. For the people who were new to the unit, as I was, our jaws dropped. He had every tab imaginable and a rack of ribbons that went to his shoulder, including Bronze and Silver Stars with "V" devices and several Purple Hearts. This humble man had been around the world and back again several times.

After drill was completed, I went to the armory bar and sat down for a cold one. My platoon sergeant walked in and said that my money wasn't good here and he would pick up my tab for today. I thanked him, and after a couple of beers I started to ask about his military career. This man was one of the first men to be in the first antiterrorist subunit of the Green Berets in Vietnam, called Blue Light. That day, I met a man who changed my life forever.

Before I departed to go back to college, I asked him what the secret to his success in the Army was. His reply was short and to the point. He said, "Show up on time and in the right uniform, and you have half the battle won." He also explained that if you study and practice your field craft and are familiar with what everyone else is doing to support you, "you can wing the rest."

So there it is, folks: words from a highly trained and educated special operations operator. Show up on time and in the right uniform, and you have half the battle won.

13

Where Credit Is Due

Sometimes taking credit for a job well done is only part of being a leader. Give credit to those who planned and executed the plan.

I hate hearing officers and senior NCOs take credit for mission success when they sat in the tent or a vehicle watching everyone else complete the mission and then moved on to the next one. I never really understood why these leaders took credit for everyone else's work—or not until I was given an award for top reconnaissance surveillance occupation of position (RSOP) team.

I was the leader of the ten-member team and had been training for months, but all the time and effort paid off when the commander requested my presence in his office. I was quite proud of our accomplishments and was not shy about telling others, but that night in the old man's office, he asked my opinion about whom we should we give awards. The commander said he was going to give three awards, and he wanted to know who should receive them. He then further clarified his remarks, saying that I could chose only two people for the awards, as I was going to get the first one. I very respectfully declined the award, suggesting that it be given to one more of my subordinates.

For a reason which I only later understood, he got mad at my refusing his award. I told him we were a team, and everyone played a part in executing each phase of the operation. He listened to my plight, but to no avail—nothing changed. He asked, Who wrote the operations order? Who gave the safety brief? Who facilitated the sand table? Who briefed the plan to the headquarters? And who took the scolding when the team didn't do everything on time? The answer to all those questions was me; I was the one who did all of those things so that the NCOs could do other things, and I ultimately was in charge and would have to accept success or failure.

At that moment I finally understood why I was getting the highest award and what the leaders in my past were actually doing. The person in the vehicle was driving around ensuring that the movement plan was being executed on time and in the right order, and the commander in the tent was monitoring communications and directing fires to other places while verifying our locations on the map board. Things as they appear may not be what you think, as it is a matter of perspective.

From that day forward, whenever I received an award, I always accepted it, but on behalf of those who helped and completed the mission, and always using "we" instead of "I." I guess I will always have a little angst for taking credit for other team members' work, so when I'm in charge, I always recognize the entire team and their efforts.

Dr. Mark P. Michels, LTC, USA (ret)

Vision and Intent

Always provide a clear vision and intent; in the absence of a leader, work will go on.

Always providing a clear vision and intent may seem an evident thing for a leader to do, but that couldn't be further from what actually happens. The fact is, most people don't know what they want or have a hard time communicating their intent to others. In the military's formal schooling for noncommissioned, warrant, and commissioned officers, candidates spend several days teaching and learning about making clear mission statements and visions with key tasks through theory, practical applications, and peer reviews. Why do these schools dedicate two to three days to vision and intent? Because it is extremely important! Approving a mission statement and key tasks is formalized in service-specific planning models and joint publications. Once a planning staff gets an approved mission statement or vision, it sets the stage for everything else. Without this information, a planning staff wouldn't know who was supposed to do what, where, when, how, and for what purpose. This valuable information must be codified at the lowest levels.

Since a leader can't be everywhere at once, understanding mission requirements and vision are paramount when he or she isn't around. For instance, say the CEO of your law firm wanted to expand the firm to new locations and needed a new marketing plan. Your job as Chief Operating Officer is to help the planning staff to develop a new marketing strategy for different locations. You have a very experienced staff, and they developed three possible new locations based on the number of arrests per county. The analysis was completed. But knowing the CEO's intent and vision, you as the planning facilitator and COO had the group start on finding suitable building spaces and creating a detailed cost sheet for the movement and occupation budget.

In this scenario, why didn't you just tell the staff to go home after they completed the original goal? The answer is that you understood the intent and vision of the CEO and knew what steps to continue planning to achieve the intent. In the absence of leaders, understanding intent and mission requirements will allow for continued progress without leadership intervention 100 percent of the time.

15

Keep Calm and Carry On

What separates good leaders from great leaders is how they plan, guide, and execute actions designed to fix bad situations.

In many cases, when things go wrong, the staff already have contingency plans to mitigate the situation, or someone from higher up will dictate actions for you to execute. However, if you find yourself in a situation without a ready contingency plan or someone from higher headquarters issuing new orders, your next move will define you as a leader to your supervisors, peers, and subordinates alike.

Now that I'm retired and consulting for businesses, I tell the C-level staff that when something goes wrong, a knee-jerk reaction is usually not the right answer. The C staff look at me and want an immediate answer, but my reply will always be the same. As long as no one is getting killed, and no bullets are flying overhead or mortars coming in, we take a tactical pause and develop a plan to fix the problem. I can't tell you how many times this happens in everyday life in the military, whether you're in garrison and you are the staff duty on call, or you're the convoy commander when the GPS isn't working and you have eighteen clicks left to travel. Stuff happens all the time, and your ability to deal with the situation calmly and in a methodical manner will be tested.

Depending on the timeliness of the decision required, I ask myself four very quick questions and then write down the answers.

1. What are we supposed to do, and by when?
2. What happened to prevent us from accomplishing this task?
3. Who needs to know what is happening?
4. Who can help develop mitigation measures based on the current situation?

After writing down the answers, I gather the necessary people who I think would add value to the discussion in one place. During that discussion, I repeat the first two questions and explain to whom I sent the information for situational awareness. Then I explain to the people assembled that they will help develop a plan to fix the situation.

Odds are, if you have selected the right people to attend your planning meeting, they will have an idea already or will have experienced the same situation previously and be able to contribute to a viable solution. No matter what happens, even if you are a mess inside, try to appear calm and collected. If you appear flustered, your internal angst will snowball and make planning efforts worse, and bad decisions could be made.

With time and a lot of practice, staying calm during stressful situations will become easier. More important, this skill is essential so that others are confident in your leadership abilities.

Dr. Mark P. Michels, LTC, USA (ret)

16

Be Compassionate

Some situations require a leader to be sensitive and compassionate. Your supervisors, peers, and subordinates will notice and thank you for it.

Not all good deeds go noticed, but some do. Some leaders are quick to punish and move on, but the fact of the matter is that punishments don't always fix the problem the person has or had. This leadership point is hard to explain without giving an example.

Here's one clear example from my time as a platoon leader stationed at Fort Bliss, Texas. I found out that one of the senior NCOs was having problems at home and had difficulties making it to work on time in the morning. The NCO had to find childcare and shuttle his children to and from day care without the help of his spouse. Situations like this happen, but the military childcare plan is only required of single parents or dual military families, not when the spouse leaves the home. Now that the spouse of this NCO had left the home, he now was required to make a family care plan for his children, which takes time, money, and a bit of legal work.

This adjustment was rather difficult for him, and he needed time to fix the situation. During the week this happened, his number came up for twenty-four-hour weekend staff duty NCO. I didn't ask if he wanted me to take his duty. I just made a phone call and added myself to the roster in his place. I had the current staff duty call him to cancel his staff duty for the weekend, and I told them to schedule me in his place for the next month. I overheard him ask the staff duty why they canceled his duty, but I made sure the staff duty just said they were instructed to do so. I took my staff duty and his for the next eight weeks. He knew I took his duty but never said anything, nor did I expect him to.

Then came his permanent change of station (PCS) move party. Everyone gets together for these parties and has a couple of drinks, and we share a big meal with others. During his speech, he paused for a second then called me out by name, thanking me for what I had done for him in the time of his need. He explained how having the time to spend with his children, making legal appointments, and solidifying childcare resources also gave him the time to get an approved family care plan, thus allowing him to continue his service in the Army.

The speech he made that night encouraged others to help those people in need or less fortunate than themselves. Don't forget the important adage "Mission first, and men always."

Dr. Mark P. Michels, LTC, USA (ret)

17

Share the Info

Always ask yourself, What information do I have that others require? Never hold information just to have it for yourself.

It is not uncommon for people to become aware that individuals with whom they work have hoarded information. In today's information exchange, it is rather easy to get overwhelmed with the number of tweets, posts, and emails full of valuable and not so valuable information. However, when a communiqué is discovered that may or may not affect other people, it is important to let them know about that information.

Here's a situation I ran into during a field exercise. A certain person spoke with the Brigade Operations Officer on the side after the formal briefing was conducted and received some information that the briefers had failed to speak about. No one in the audience had caught the omission, so this person was the only one besides the planning staff to have the additional information.

Some of you reading this may blame the Operations Officer for the lack of communication, but normally, as separate batteries, we as the lower leaders shared information daily while in the field. For some reason, though, this person did not share the extra information he had with anyone.

So there we were, five batteries moving though the desert at night, and the path we chose to travel was cut off with enemy activity.

We had to chose an alternate route. Normally during traveling, planning for primary and secondary routes was standard procedure, so like clockwork we diverted the entire convoy on the secondary route onto a short stretch of the route parallel to the main highway. Such a situation required near blackout conditions on the highway as the dust clouds bellowed over the road and underpasses. Everything might have been fine, except that it hadn't rained in Texas for a very long time, and dust storms had become quite common.

It did not take long for civilian highway travelers to call 911 and the news of what we were doing to make its way back to my vehicle. Every battery that got hit took a similar route next to the highway, except for one. When the Brigade Commander stopped chewing the battalion commanders' asses, I overheard the Operations Officer make a radio call to the person to whom he had given the additional information. Apparently, this missing information was that all traffic for day and night was not to travel on the trail next to the highway because of the dust.

Because of one person's inability to share information, a major highway was shut down, police man-hours were increased, negative media coverage was given, and I'm sure a couple of counseling statements were delivered. I do know that the person who withheld the information was denied any extensions of service.

No matter what type of information this person had, it was important for others to know and understand it. If this information had been shared, it would have saved some scolding, counseling statements, policeman hours, blocked traffic, and a military career.

There's No Such Thing as Drudge Work

Sometimes learning to "paint rocks" has a moral or learning objective.

It has been several years since the Army required boots to be highly shined and uniforms to be ironed. When I was a lower enlisted soldier, I thought to myself that shining boots and ironing my uniform was a big waste of time. But when I became a senior NCO, I was able to step back and observe people and their time-management skills. Soldiers who had a regimented schedule for shining their boots and ironing their uniform after work also showed up to work on time and for the most part were more disciplined than soldiers who didn't shine their boots and iron their uniforms.

Carrying out the same tasks regularly, like checking email as soon as you get to work, can save you from many heartaches and problems later. I try not to work on the weekends if I don't have to, but old habits are hard to break. On occasion, a vender cancelled appointments or deliveries were delayed, which required quick movement of appointment time slots and various resources required to be modified. If I were not regimented to do the same thing every morning, I would have missed the email and quite possibly lost money for the customer.

The person requiring a mundane task may be teaching you a lifetime of good habits or teaching you to develop time management skills—and you may not even realize it at the time.

Bad Examples

Sometimes it is more important to observe the people you don't want to emulate than the people you do.

Most people who give leadership talks or write books like this one explain the importance of finding a mentor you would like to emulate. The advice is sound, but I would go a step further. Besides finding the perfect mentor, find someone people don't like and try to figure out why. How do they interact with others? What is it that people do not like? Is it their personality, lack of knowledge, poor program management skills, or something else? Once you think you know, take this knowledge and try never to do what others dislike about this person. My use of the word "never" is kind of loose, though, so I'll explain.

If people don't like this person for exposing wrongdoing, cheating, or dishonesty, then take the dislike for this person as a badge of honor. However, if you have determined that people don't like this person for reasons other than being honorable and honest, then it is your turn to help this person become better. That's right—I said to help them be a better person. If the person lacks people skills, help others understand the person. If the person lacks institutional knowledge, help educate the person. Whatever characteristic this person lacks, if they are willing to accept help, your job is to provide it.

This person just might turn around and become one of the unit's or company's greatest assets because of your assistance. The world is full of great people who lacked leadership and program management skills at one time. Take steps to help these people, and give them a second chance to become a better leader or manager.

20

Lessons Learned

Always search for leadership Lessons Learned (L2) documents and insight or other historical closeout reports (CRs) and refer to them as planning tools. L2s and CRs are as important to leaders as planning subject-matter experts are.

Most industries have a repository for past performance in email strings, after-action reviews, or closeout reports. Researching documents to find out what people did in the past in regard to specific events will be worth the time.

When I was in the service, I was a part of the Lesson Learned Program, which observed exercises and conducted interviews with people to find "sustains" and "improves." The sample group was always carefully selected, as some people have more visibility regarding how operations are conducted than others. Not to say that everyone didn't have an opinion, but the private siting by the radio delivering messages in the tactical operations center did not have a complete picture of what everyone was doing.

However, if we had time, I would interview these people, and to my surprise, they almost always had an interesting view of the exercise. These codified observations—good and bad—were always made public for the military personnel to see so that others could learn about the progress or setbacks that people before them had.

Why is this important? Sometimes these observations can lead to developing trends and gaps that can be addressed to increase capability and/or capacity. It stands to reason that you should learn from the mistakes of others as you prepare to innovative ways to carry out the same actions. Nobody likes to make the same mistake twice. Learn from others; your supervisors, peers, and subordinates will thank you for it.

21

Give Yourself a Break

Know when to take a break, because eventually you will be forced to.

There was a time in my early military career when it was a badge of honor to carry thirty days of leave over to the next fiscal year. I was content with the military holiday leave schedules and three- or four-day passes, which were provided without my having to use up my leave balance. I was on a very fast-moving train, and I was afraid that if I wasn't there to contribute, I would be left out of the planning process.

Early in my officer career, I was in a field exercise and was on the early planning staff and advance party. The first day started with the execution of the recall at 0330 hours, and for the next three days out of eight, all we did was set up, become mission ready, and move again. In four days, I think we moved five times.

I was also in charge of planning and executing the reconnaissance plan for each new position and setup. You can imagine after I got the unit to 100 percent mission ready, I tried to get some sleep. However, it seemed that whenever I found an empty vehicle seat to sleep on, another movement order arrived, and the planning and execution cycle repeated itself yet again.

On the fourth day, an evaluator gave my crew and me a table 8 proficiency drill on the firing sequence and air battle. After passing the table drill, the evaluator provided us a back brief … and I fell asleep sitting in front of him. I was embarrassed, but all he did was to provide me with an exercise casualty card.[2] I magically had wounds that required me to be evacuated immediately to the rear for a day and a half before I could return to the field exercise.

I didn't say much, only handed my card to my NCO, who went into action. But I did manage to corner the evaluator outside, asking him why the injury card and not something less time consuming. His answer to me was nothing but questions.

Wasn't I the first to arrive at the unit during recall?

Wasn't I there for every meeting and change over?

Was I the person briefing the movement plans and safety plans on every move?

Wasn't I the one on every reconnaissance mission of position and responsible for mission readiness?

My answer to him every time was yes. Then it dawned on me that he and the other evaluators were teaching me a valuable lesson, as was the Battery Commander. They wanted to see how long I could keep up my pace without jeopardizing the mission. The casualty card forced the Battery Commander to pick someone else to conduct the recon, movement, and mission planning along with the table 8 drills. The evaluator made several valid points, and I was forced not to participate in the exercise—and slept for quite possibly the best four to five hours that I had in a very long time. I felt like a new man.

Later in my career, when my positions entailed more desk work, I found myself doing the same thing. Mentally, I felt exhausted. I missed the outdoors, where I could work with my hands and interact with soldiers daily but with more rank and responsibility. I kept the same schedule for a long time, until my wife and I had two children in diapers and one just in a beginner car seat. This family situation changed my perspective on what taking time off really meant.

---

[2] Exercise casualty cards come in a deck the size of regular playing cards. They describe types of injuries or illnesses on one side and show areas of the body affected on the other.

Not taking leave was no longer a badge of honor, as it became a requirement to help raise our children. I have been in combat arms and combat support for most of my military career, and I have spent years deployed, on temporary duty, or in the field, leaving my wife to raise our children by herself. Taking leave now was not for *me*; it was for my family, and to give my wife a break so she could just go out with her friends, attend a church prayer group, go shopping alone, or help clean the house. Taking leave ensured she had time for herself. This was now the focus of my time off.

22

Human Insight

Leaders must remember that people are human and have mental and physical needs, wants, and desires. Understanding human nature can help leaders provide incentives or punishment.

Sometimes being shortsighted and task-oriented is a good thing, when short deadlines are coming up fast or an emergency rises. However, such behaviors should not be the norm. The norm should be careful planning efforts by leaders and staff. Learning what your supervisors, peers, and subordinates respond to is essential. There are three motivators—three reasons or influences—that affect behavior, and these typically coincide with age or experience, though there will always be individual exceptions. The first is avoidance of pain. The second is regulation or laws. The third is fear of disappointment.

Generally speaking, young people in their college years, or the military equivalent of ranks E-1 through E-4, usually respond to money and time. They like three- and four-day passes, or in the workplace, a nice bonus or increased responsibility as a challenge. This rule is not hard and fast, but in my experience, if someone gets in trouble at this age, taking time and money from them usually produces the desired behavior.

For working-class civilians, and in the military E-5 through E-7 personnel and the ranks of second lieutenant through captain

(2LT–CPT), "bad paper" usually moves efforts in the direction you need. "Bad paper" is nonjudicial punishment, in particular certain levels of permanent or on station only letters that may or may not stay in a person's file for others to see and may inhibit one's career. At this level, people are more likely to respond to positive reinforcement than negative.

When dealing with how to provide future direction for senior personnel, consider where they are on the ladder. High-ranking people—in the military, a major, lieutenant colonel, first sergeant, or sergeant major; in the corporate hierarchy, a vice president or chief operating officer—know their worth and are usually the go-to people when emergencies arise. People at this level in life have made a long-term commitment to whatever they are doing and typically will be motivated by knowing they made a difference. They require hardly any negative written counseling and respond to other people's success. Allowing these people to see the results of hard work is even better than saying "good job," because they know it is their job and successful execution is thanks enough. When for some reason these people are not performing well, a short one-on-one office call provides enough feedback to follow the yellow brick road—*if* they respect you. If not, there is always reassignment or the unemployment line.

23

Find Your Voice

If you don't have a voice, you will never be heard.

This statement seems common sense, but to my chagrin, it is not. Depending on your personality, position, or location, having a voice may not be an option for a myriad of reasons. But it doesn't mean your ideas or thoughts do not have merit. How many times have you been doing your normal job when your supervisor says, "The way we do things will be changing"? The resulting feelings may cause discontent or even resentment.

For me, it happened a lot in the military, but I knew my place. I knew that someday I would be the decision maker, and I could be the one to make changes. I just had to wait my turn. As I progressed in the military, I found out that some or most new actions were calculated and planned out at various levels and were otherwise directed change. I didn't know this when I was early in my career. I just knew I had to do things differently from the day before. Some actions were better than others. Nonetheless, I learned that if the change made what I did less effective and efficient, I needed to speak up. But when I did, I had to prove my statement of disproval. I usually had to time the actions, demonstrate them, and provide a solution once I understood the intent of the change.

This valuable lesson was one I learned early on and still use in my consulting business. It is not good enough to say that something is wrong or doesn't work correctly. You have to prove it in a way that the decision maker can best understand. Don't be surprised if even after you present overwhelming evidence for changing something back or modifying a change, it does not get implemented. There can be many reasons this happens—such as personal pride, direction from a superior, or some kind of personal vendetta. However, if you don't say anything, you will have to live with the outcome for better or worse.

But when safety is involved, always—and I mean always—say something. I don't care where you are in the military ranks or civilian workforce, saying something that may save someone's life is always a requirement. You never know when having a voice and being heard may have made a process more effective and efficient—or potentially may save someone's life.

Dr. Mark P. Michels, LTC, USA (ret)

24

The Right Speed

Fast is slow, and slow is fast.

There are people in this world who can read an instruction manual or observe a one-time demonstration and repeat the process without batting an eye. I am not one of those people. I have to read something at least twice and put my hands on whatever I'm trying to do several times a day to make sure I don't do something wrong. If you are like me, then this leadership quote is for you.

I first heard this quote in Rappel Master School. I didn't understand what it meant until we got into the hands-on inspection phase of the curriculum. We had to inspect three people in various equipment prior to conducting rappelling operations. We had to do a proper inspection and find all the discrepancies to pass. For the first two people, I found the mistakes without looking very hard, and I stuck to the "by the numbers" process which made finding the discrepancies easy. Then I got to the third person.

I started as usual. I spotted a discrepancy within the first ten seconds, but when I called it out, I lost my place in the proper sequence and started to jump around looking for the last two discrepancies. I managed to find one more but failed to find the last one and had to go back to the end of the line for retraining.

Since I had rocked the first two inspections, I didn't know what I had done wrong on the third until the senior instructor came up to me and said he watched me and knew the exact moment I lost my place. He said that when I saw a possible discrepancy, I got excited, lost my rhythm, and failed to pick up where I left off. He told me to remember that "fast is slow, and slow is fast." I contemplated that and finally understood what he was telling me. He meant to stick with the inspection process as demonstrated and don't deviate from it, because if you do it right the first time you will not miss the flaws.

When I got to the front of the line again, I already had three practice runs. This time I found all the discrepancies and took twenty-five seconds off my regular inspection time.

I have another example from my consulting business. I had given some young staff members a planning outline for a simple problem dealing with schedules. I gave them a step-by-step process and told them to follow it. After a short period of time, the staff members got quite good at the process—until I gave them what seemed an easy solution to the problem with a lot of variables that had to be considered. As they started to go through the planning process, they started skipping steps because they thought they already knew the outcome. When I was being briefed on the proposed solution, I asked about several of the variables, as they finished with the planning way too early to have even discussed most of the variables thoroughly. When it became evident that they had skipped sections of the planning process I gave them, they decided to go back and not skip any sections.

If the staff had gone step-by-step as instructed, they would have provided me a very detailed solution; however, by having to go back to the planning table, they wasted additional resources and time. So ... slow is fast, and fast is slow.

25

The Pie

Every leader has a piece of the pie.

Leaders and the decisions they make have varying outcomes and influences. Even the actions of a squad leader can make or break a tactical operation.

In my travels as a Lesson Learned observer and contributor, I ran across a young officer I interviewed regarding past actions on an objective. One of the comments he made stands out in my memory: he felt his actions didn't really matter to the outcome of the larger operation. At first, I thought that his leadership had failed to provide the "big picture" in briefings or in the operations order, so I asked him various questions. His answers were spot-on, according to the briefings and order that I had read, so he knew what he was supposed to do and why. So failure of the chain of command to inform him of his mission was null.

After several more questions, it dawned on me that he was good at his job and was a good leader but just didn't get the big picture and how his little team's actions influenced an entire theater's defense posture. This officer and his team found materials and information that changed the PPE posture in the operation. After his team came back from the operation, information did not flow back down again until his team was needed elsewhere, so there was a communication break. He had no idea it was his team that helped shape the decision. As far as he and his team were concerned, they just did their job and that was it, nothing more. This couldn't have been farther from the truth. I told him the influence his team had, and he became a different person with a different attitude.

Think of mission accomplishment as a whole pie. The generals have larger pieces, and the lower your rank, the smaller your piece is. But you still get a piece of pie. Without every person doing their job and adding to the pie, the mission would never be complete. No matter how big the mission is and how small your piece of pie is within it, the mission will not be complete until everyone contributes.

Make a Difference

No matter what you do, just make a difference.

Finding your way in life is important. Without having direction, you would be wandering around this world aimlessly, with no purpose. When I was young, my parents told me that they didn't care what I did in life; they just wanted to see me happy. I didn't quite understand as I muddled my way through life, but I made educated guesses and committed the time and effort to see them through. I found my niche in life early on, and I thank God every month I get my military retirement check. I made the decision long ago to join the service, and thirty years later I reap the rewards.

Unfortunately, some people never really find their niche and hop from job to job looking for something that strikes their fancy. For some people it is about the money, the title, the company, or the people they help.

I have four grown children of whom I am extremely proud. I have changed my parents' saying from "Do something that makes you happy" to "Do something that makes a difference." Why the change? Throughout my life, I have met a lot of happy people who just go to a job for eight hours a day Monday through Friday and then go home. The world is full of these people, and the world needs these types of people. But their sphere of influence is limited. These are smart hardworking people who, if asked, could figure out how to move mountains. I look at these people and see huge potential wasted, but they are happy, so is it good enough.

Affecting people in a positive way, in my opinion, is making a difference. You don't have to be Mother Teresa, but using your talents to influence others in a positive way is a valuable gift to others. If you want a rewarding job or career, show up on time and in the right clothes ready to work and make a difference in people's lives. That, in my opinion, is job satisfaction.

Dr. Mark P. Michels, LTC, USA (ret)

27

Tough Inside and Out

"It is hard to look tough with tears in your eyes."

That's a quote from Richard Michels, my father, and it's saying that's been in my family for years. When someone witnesses a family member smashing a finger under a falling piece of firewood, or when someone continues working after clearly getting hurt, that's how you can expect a Michels to respond.

Now for the record, I do recommend getting checked out if you physically hurt yourself, as well as reevaluating your risk assessment. Physical toughness is only a small part of being a leader, as mental toughness is needed more often than physical. If you as a leader have work or personal issues that are affecting you, then learning to cope with them can be a hard sell to your subordinates, peers, and supervisors. The best advice I can provide is to try to compartmentalize work and non-work issues.

I know this is easier said than done, but facilitating the Agile morning stand-up meeting and breaking out in tears for no apparent reason is not acceptable professional behavior. So seek out someone who can mentor you or help find a resolution to your issue or problem—looking tough shouldn't be a show you put on but rather reflect your reality.

Be Redundant

Plan for redundancies.

If you have spent any time in the military service, this adage should be second nature. If not, a little explaining is required. Having redundancies in everything is essential in business as well as in the military. Having more than one way to communicate, store data, move, collaborate, and provide heat, food, water, and shelter is extremely important.

Here is a good example. I usually conduct my consulting business via Google Meet, but when that is not working well, I use Zoom. Having flexibility built into planning factors is a must if you want to survive in the business world.

I long have insisted on having whiteboards as status reminders so that anybody walking by can see at a glance what is happening—no need to have a computer, log in, and answer an authentication question just to get an up-to-date status. It just so happened on one field exercise that the main power went out (as instructed by the evaluators), but because we had a whiteboard that was up-to-date and not projected on a screen like those used by other sections that lost power for three to four hours, we didn't even skip a beat. After that incident, my peers and subordinates never complained about loading up my big whiteboards again.

Here is another example of how having redundancies is valuable. When I was consulting for a small business and their client documents were stored on an online server, I asked, What happens if the server goes down? How would old information be found? I suggested using CDs weekly and filing them in a fireproof case in a secure area.

It just so happened that the next week we all got an email saying they were having server problems, and we required an old client's information from a couple of years back that we could not retrieve without the server being fixed first. Having redundancies in capability and capacity is necessary.

Dr. Mark P. Michels, LTC, USA (ret)

29

Make a Decision

Not making a decision is a decision—but one that could cost you the respect required to lead.

Not every decision made by a leader is life-threatening nor requires immediacy. However, when you are the leader and the sole person to make a decision about X, Y, or Z, then *make a decision*. If you as a leader are unable to make such a decision owing to incomplete information, then your planning team didn't do a good job of presenting options, or you didn't obtain enough factual information. Your next step is to say so and to start asking pointed questions to the staff. To make a sound decision, you will require the answers to your questions.

Earlier in this book, I expounded on how important it is to ask thought-provoking questions that could steer you into a clear decision path. This is how seasoned leaders shine. I learned early in my career to think "big picture" and consider how the decisions I make affect everyone else. Sometimes, it is necessary to say, "Let me think on this, and I will provide you with a decision before the end of the day." It is perfectly acceptable, as your subordinates or staff now understand that they will be provided guidance.

The second step for the leader is to consult with an expert, whoever it may be, and to research Lessons Learned documents—again, if you have the luxury of time. If possible, be on time with your decision; don't keep the staff waiting, and don't break the one-third/two-thirds rule. (That's a standard planning formula stating that the planning staff must use only one-third of the time before execution so that people executing the plan have two-thirds of the time to prepare and rehearse prior to execution.)

Sometimes there is no right answer, but regardless of the outcome, making an informed and educated decision in a timely manner is always the right course of action.

30

The Last Word

Always speak last during meetings.

Let me explain first what I do not mean. I'm not saying to walk into a meeting and not speak to people. That would be rude.

However, after the pleasantries have been exchanged and the meeting officially starts, then it is time for you to just sit back and listen. This technique has saved me from making quick, uninformed decisions that would have turn out to be mistakes.

Many times, as the staff takes their turn briefing their part of a plan, they sometimes have changed my perspective of what I thought I knew before I walked into the meeting. This has led me to change my mind regarding a decision or guidance I would have provided without this valuable information.

So be the last to speak. And ask the right questions (see principles 5 and 6) because factual information and a plan to mitigate risks are important to making educated and sound decisions.

31

Adapt Your Style

Adapt your leadership style according to the situation at hand.

If you just started the stage of your career where you will be leading people, this principle may not come naturally. However, if you are a more seasoned leader, you will understand its importance. Whether you as a leader are authoritative, consultative, participative, laissez-faire, persuasive, transformational, or collaborative, you must be able to switch among leadership styles with ease, depending on the people you are leading.

It would be easy for me to give military examples, but let me explain leadership style flexibility in my role as a business consultant.

Usually, I report directly to the CEO, who gives me the authority to schedule meetings and make minor decisions that don't require board guidance. Once, early in the morning I received a text that required a bit more information and staffing to fix and prevent other things from happening.

When I got into the office, I walked around to one section and told them I needed everyone in the meeting room for a quick planning sprint. They knew I would never ask them to stop everything they were doing just to conduct a meeting on short notice, so I had no problem getting them to the meeting room (authoritative). When I got everyone in the room, I provided a detailed brief of what I knew, then asked for their expert knowledge and experience in solving the problem (persuasive).

As we were discussing solutions, it became evident that we had a gap in knowledge regarding a subject and needed another section to participate in the planning sprint. I quickly spoke with the section's supervisor and informed him that I required two experienced planners. After they showed up and were briefed of the situation, it was immediately clear that these were the people who could help solve the problem (authoritative and collaborative).

As the planning went on, I sensed that some of the staff members were not used to the formal planning style I use and teach, so I rolled up my sleeves, figuratively, and walked the less-experienced people through the formal planning process (participative). The staff seemed to be moving along and developed some feasible plans of action, so I asked each person their thoughts on each course of action, and to my surprise most of the staff agreed (consultative). When the planning was complete, I gathered up the key planners and briefed the CEO on the plan to mitigate the problem.

In the course of three and a half hours of meetings, I used five leadership styles.

It may take time to learn to switch among leadership styles, but when you get it right, your staff, peers, and subordinates will notice your flexibility to adapt in stressful situations when they arise, and they will thank you.

32

Courage

Have courage—people don't like leaders who are cowards.

There are several forms of courage—not limited to mental, moral, and physical courage—but the courage I'm talking about here is the willingness to try something different, after some planning, and see if it works. There is nothing worse than a status quo leader. If different paths aren't blazed, progress will never be made; eventually, your efforts will stagnate, and progress becomes nonexistent. If you have provided your staff with the facts and worked through assumptions, having the courage to do something no one has done before can be exciting.

When I transitioned from enlisted to a commissioned officer, I had to attend a summer camp in Washington state. During the field phase, it came my turn to lead a mission. I set up a close ambush, but not in the normal L shape that is taught in infantry school. I was issued two claymore mines and a lot of crew-served weapon ammunition. As I briefed my plan, it was funny watching cadets get confused when I didn't follow normal small unit tactics. I thought their heads were going to explode.

The intelligence I received was that a platoon-plus element was walking down the road, and I had twenty minutes to set up an ambush. My instructions were simple: place one claymore at the bend of the road facing the straight path; line both sides of the road in the ditches with detonation cord; place interlocking fire on the kill zone.

Suffice it to say that by the time the claymore simulator went off and the crew-served weapons started sounding off, only a handful of the opposing force made it into the ditches on either side of the road, at which point I called for setting off the det cord.

Unbeknown to me, the senior officer assigned to mentor me had placed a net call for other instructors to watch what would happen. The result ended in 100 percent mission accomplishment in less than fifteen seconds.

I could've just done the L-shaped ambush like everyone else, but I had the courage to try something different, and luckily for me, it worked great.

Dr. Mark P. Michels, LTC, USA (ret)

Slow But Steady Wins the Race

If you can't be quick, be dependable.

Through my career, I have seen some very smart people, and some who, let's say, needed more training. But in many cases, the smart people had mixed results for delivering documents on time or completing tasks.

During the planning phase of supporting a national special security event, I usually got two planners from each section to join the planners group. When I got to know everyone among the planners, I would assign writing tasks or PowerPoint slide requirements to a specific person, depending on my time requirements. If I needed something quickly but knew I had to review it for mistakes, I knew whom to assign. Conversely, if I had a lot of time before I had to turn in the finished product, I chose the person I knew would take longer to write the section but would make fewer mistakes. Mistakes are inevitable, but I would rather have a "just in time" product that is accurate with few or no mistakes than something speedy but riddled with errors.

So I would much rather give a task to someone who might take longer to complete it than to someone quick-minded who is less dependable. For example, if the task were to develop a document or brief, the person who is more dependable might require a little more document editing or a little more training on a manual task. But consistency is an important planning factor in ensuring timeliness and predictability.

34

Build on Strengths, Manage Weaknesses

Understand everyone's strengths and weaknesses—everyone has them.

In some sense, we are not all created equal. People have different skills, and complete tasks at different rates.

I'm reminded of a time when I was at Joint Task Force–Civil Support (JTF-CS) and we were contending with a real-life situation. I was the chief facilitator of the planning session, and we had very little time to develop and present a plan. There are many functions that had to be completed to finish the specific plan, but I knew I was good at the big picture and could draw it on the whiteboard.

Now, I know my writing is hard to read, so I was not going to take notes while I was facilitating, nor was I going to make modifications to the operation plan (OPLAN) or make PowerPoint slides. I am weak in these areas, so I asked some of the planning staff to take charge of these functions. They knew what their strengths were, and they knew mine. To be honest, they would have volunteered anyway, as we worked well together.

Could I have made the PowerPoint slides? Yes. Could I have made the modification to the OPLAN? Certainly. But acknowledging one another's strengths and weaknesses made developing a plan a lot easier, and resulted in very few modifications after the first briefing. Knowing the strengths and weaknesses of everyone on your team is beneficial for any planning development effort—and for everyday life.

35

Trust Must Be Earned

Trust but verify.

This lesson took me some time to understand fully. During my time as an enlisted soldier, I observed my peers and supervisors do what they said they were going to do—and, with only a very few exceptions, everything was done on time. But when I started to work at the two- and three-star levels, I found out that senior field-grade officers eat their own.

One day, a planning effort had gone directly from the Major General to my colonel to me. I was a junior major at the time but had a lot of experience in the area the plan was focused on, so I gathered my staff and was put on a strict schedule to ensure the initial brief would happen in a timely manner. Every person I requested came to participate in the planning efforts, except for one section. I didn't have time to track anyone down. After the first planning meeting, I met up with the colonel responsible for the missing section.

With all the notes that we had from planning, as well as a draft brief, I conducted a brief presentation and explained what I needed help with. After some short questions, the colonel stated that his section would provide the required information two hours prior to the brief so I could add his part of the general's brief.

So there I am, a junior major being told by a full-bird colonel that he would make sure I would have his section's material before the brief. Every section provided me with their slides three hours prior to the brief, which I was then able to complete—except that the colonel who had told me he would provide the information required for his section did not do so on time.

I placed the staff on a fifteen-minute break before the final rehearsal and checked my email for the promised documents. Nothing in my inbox. I then went to my colonel and told him that I didn't have what the other section's colonel had promised. I relayed the direct conversation I'd had with the other colonel, and explained that their brief was now late. He advised me to go to the section and see what the holdup was.

I went to the section, and immediately someone met me at the door and told me they were instructed not to provide the slides. What to do?

Well, I went back to the main brief, and for every slide that the section was required to put information in, I entered "failed to provide information."

During the brief, as soon as the first slide with "failed to provide information" came up, the General asked me several questions. I told him what I had requested and what the section's leadership replied directly to me. After the brief was completed, the general asked me to stay behind—along with the colonel who had been responsible for providing me the information.

First, the general commended me for the planning effort, but then he left me with a piece of advice. He said, "You trust people too much and expect others to be honorable and live up to their word as you do. In the future, to ensure timeliness you need to trust but verify other people's deliverables that they owe you."

I thanked general for the advice, rendered a salute, did an about-face, and exited the room. As soon as I closed the door, a very strong one-way conversation happened.

When people promise you something, remember: trust, but verify in a timely manner.

36

Find the Motivation

False motivation is better than no motivation.

When you are a leader, people look to you for support and guidance. There are going to be days on occasion—because of life, basically—that you are going to go into work not feeling it. If you find yourself in one of these days, walk into work and try to be normal. Walk around the office, say hello, and ask how their day is going. Ask your managers some not-so-detailed question about an effort they oversee. You're just looking for a short answer, not a complete brief, so frame your question with that in mind.

After you make your rounds, look at the meeting schedule. Here is the most important step: *stop what you are doing, sit back in your chair, and do* nothing *for at least five minutes.* Collect yourself. If you can, instruct your gatekeeper not to allow anyone in your office for up to twenty minutes. Take this time to gather yourself and relax. Just don't relax too much—you still have the rest of the day to work!

When you have a bad day, your supervisors, peers, or subordinates should not be able to tell. I say this with one caveat: if you have a peer at work whom you can trust or who has a motivating influence on you, then try to take an off-site lunch with this person, and ask that they keep your conversation to themselves. Motivation is contagious, so spread the wealth.

According to Plan

"When things don't go as planned, look in the mirror first."

—Edward (Stan) Bacon,
JTF-CS Deputy J5,
US Marine Corps Maj (Ret.)

Stan Bacon was a retired Marine and a strict process-driven person who worked as the deputy director of the Plans section. He knew the joint planning process through and through and held you to the standard. If things did not go as planned, he would often times call for a self-reflection—the mirror. Mistakes happen, but if you make the same mistake twice, then the mistake looks squarely back at you.

But as a leader, you must realize that most plans don't survive first contact. You probably could find someone, or many people, to blame for the failure—but don't. Step back and ask yourself, "Did I provide the required intent, vision, or key tasks?" Then ask yourself, "Did the staff, along with my guidance, plan for, try to identify, and mitigate risk with contingency efforts?"

If you can't answer yes to these questions, then you have yourself to blame. Learn from your mistakes, and ask important questions (see principles 5 and 6) to make your planners begin to think, act, react, and counter-act for phase planning. The same methods for planning can be used in the corporate world.

38

Your Good Name

> **"The most important thing you wear on your uniform is your name tag."**
> —MSG Ray Loos, US Army MSG (Ret.)

For a little more than thirty years, my daily uniform had a US Army tag on one side and my name on the other. I've always remembered a conversation I had when I was on recruiting duty with my mentor, Ray Loos. Ray was an E-7 SFC back then, and a very well-respected, hardworking soldier at the Syracuse Army Recruiting Station. He taught me how to talk to people on the fly and how to budget my time more effectively. I have carried lessons I learned from him through my entire career.

Here's the lesson that most stands out to me. One night after work, we were having a couple of drinks at a bar (recruit prospecting) and started discussing some recruiter improprieties that came to light in a neighboring station. The topic quickly turned to ethics and pride. Then-SFC Loos stated that I should always remember that everything I did and failed to do would be associated with the name on my uniform. People will not remember that I was a recruiter or a rappel master—just my name.

Later that night, I pondered what he had said. Then it dawned on me that he was teaching me much more than just the significance of my name tag on my uniform. He was teaching me about the importance of who I am as a person: how I treat people, how I lead them, how I react to stress.

Wherever we work, at a bank or Google or anywhere else, the world is full of evil temptation. Only those who are ethically strong and morally grounded will not be persuaded to do wrong. You can do a hundred things right, but do one thing wrong, and they will remember you for it as clearly as the name on your uniform.

39

Dream for Reality

Don't follow your dream (unless it is practical); do something now that will benefit you later.

I'm sure you've heard the advice to do something you enjoy as a career. Or you may have heard people offer this bit of advice: find a career that suits your personality. Hogwash!

I say do something practical that earns you a very good living from—something that allows you to build up a "nest egg" and develop a skill or trade. The world is full of starving artists and liberal arts majors with dashed hopes, but the truth is that not many people can earn a steady income by making paintings or sculptures or reading books. The exceptions are far and few between.

This is the advice I gave in providing the required counseling to my soldiers when they expressed their intention of leaving the Army. Some people join the Army as a steppingstone to get somewhere else, and that's OK. But for those people who joined the service and then want to leave to follow their dream, the dream should be practical or well thought out.

Here is a great example of using the military as a steppingstone to better oneself. I worked as a consultant for a law firm and found out that one of the attorneys had been in the Army. He joined the Army to become a special operator, but because of an injury, his training was cut short. However, he continued to work hard and make payments to his GI Bill monthly.

He always wanted to be an attorney. So after his service obligation was up, he left the Army and went to law school using his GI Bill. With the GI bill paying for his college, and other service-related scholarships, he graduated law school virtually free of debt.

In another example, I was counseling a soldier about leaving the Army, a young man who wanted to get out and become a counselor or something along these lines, as I recall. OK, before I get hate mail, some counselors are paid well, in some cities in the US. However, these positions are usually earmarked for an internal employee with substantial time in the career, not for a newbie. This soldier was trained to fuel every piece of equipment we had, take fuel samples, and conduct the analysis, as well as to maintain automated and manual records. This guy was great; he was dependable and always willing to help others in need.

My recommendation to him was to take additional certifications while he was still in the military and to use them to get a really good job while working on his passion part-time. He took my advice and reenlisted for a short time. I did my best to allow him to attend every school he could go to, as long as he mentored others. He eventually exited the Army, and in less than two weeks, while on his terminal leave, he got a part-time position at the airport, working half the hours he did in the Army and at a rate of compensation more than three times his Army pay.

About six months after he got out, I ran into him as I was walking to my truck in the airport parking lot. He had longer hair and a mustache, but he was the same hardworking person I knew from before. He thanked me for the advice and the extra schooling he was allowed to attend. I'm not sure if he ever became whatever his dream job was, but he sure seemed happy.

40

Praise and Punishment

Praise in public but discipline in private.

This principle does not apply to situations requiring formal mental and physical indoctrination of the sort that some of you who joined the service or another agency may have experienced. Even then, you may recall that as time went on, universal punishment eventually gave way to a more individual approach.

Operationalizing this principle will gain you a lot of respect as a leader, if you remain consistent in its intent. Providing a parking spot for employee of the month, a bonus to the highest-selling salespeople in a company, or giving an accommodation medal in front of peers, subordinates, and supervisors can increase morale and esprit de corps within an organization—if it is justly earned.

Conversely, when you know you did something wrong, hearing "the commander wants to see you" or "see the boss before you go home" is rarely a good thing. The military does execute punishment in public, as nonjudicial punishment has to be posted in public places and stripes are lost in formation sometimes. But I would like to think that this is the exception and not the rule.

Putting Failures behind You

Don't let your past mistakes destroy your potential future.

So many people live in the past and can't quite shake it off. You may have failed a semester in college, got arrested, said something to a loved one that you shouldn't have … we all have done things we are not proud of. What you should not do is let it affect you to the point of inhibiting you in making positive changes in your life.

I've lived in the Army of "zero defect," and I could see how risk-adverse leadership affected mission accomplishment. Quite honestly, it was a boring time during which the Army did not have much growth in industry and technical advancements, in my opinion.

Over time, the Army adopted a more "let's try it" mantra and started to grow more, especially at the beginning of and during a war. With people and resource shortages, leaders had to become resourceful and thrifty. This type of environment brings out the entrepreneurs, inventors, and out-of-the-box thinkers. The "let's try it" environment is a perfect opportunity to forget the sins of the past and move out smartly. Eventually people will forget who you were and what you did, so move on!

Now, I'm not going to tell you that every bad deed can be undone, nor should it be. Punishment is meant to remind you of what you did and to act as a deterrent not to repeat that. Punishment is a necessary evil. But if you have trouble overcoming your internal struggles, seek a counselor, mentor, or a member of the clergy for religious guidance—people formally trained to counsel people in distress. Make a goal or a plan, and move out smartly, leaving your failures in the past and concentrating on the path ahead.

Think First

"Don't let your feet outrun your brain."

This was a frequent saying from my grandmother Thola Michels to my father when he was young, and he has passed it on.

One day, while helping my father cut down trees, chunk them up, split them, and stack them, my daughter backed up the truck full of wood and stopped about fifteen feet from where the wood pile was. Without a second thought, my wife and our son started to unload the back of the truck.

Meanwhile, my father and I were using the wood splitter. We looked at each other, and each of us immediately knew what the other was thinking. When my daughter came out of the truck, my father said to her, "Don't let your feet outrun your brain." She looked puzzled, and I pointed to her mother and brother walking back and forth fifteen feet to stack the wood. My daughter looked at me and smiled, so I just said, "Tell them to move out of the way, and back the truck up to the pile."

If you have lived on a farm or cut wood, I'm sure you can confirm that if you don't do things very often, you need to shake the dust off before you become proficient again. This short example and family saying can be applied to many situations.

As a leader, why would you do things just because they have been done that way? Always look for better efficiency and capacity. Someday you might be stuck with very few resources and be forced to streamline a process. Why wait? Always look for ways to streamline a process. Just keep in mind that streamlining is not the same thing as cutting corners; for example, sections of a process might require a timed delay, such as working with chemicals or allowing material to dry.

If you really want to understand what Grandma Michels was trying to convey, take a Lean Six Sigma class. However, when you are cutting wood to heat the house, "Don't let your feet outrun your brain" works just as well.

43

Share the Knowledge

Teach or mentor someone to do what you do.

As a leader, if you are a single point of failure, then you already have missed the mark on your duty to teach. Teaching or mentoring people to do your job doesn't mean you give away your decision-making authority—you're just delegating the process. Teach someone, or several people, to do the work you do in your absence.

Of course, there will be times when you still get a call while on vacation, because emergencies do happen. However, if these types of calls are not rare, you are failing to leave proper guidance.

Think about what we do as leaders at work: we provide guidance, documents, briefs, or analyses, depending on what is required and what type of leader you are. It is your responsibility to provide your staff with the necessary tools, documents, and guidance prior to your departure. If you know you are going on vacation or a short getaway, finding a person you trust should be relatively easy, given advance notice. However, unexpected deaths or accidents do happen and require a leader's quick attention. For these situations, having someone who has your trust and confidence to take over for you is paramount. If you have failed to train someone, it should not be a surprise to you that your staff calls you during and off work hours.

Take an hour or two to mentor someone every week and show them what you do and why. Sometimes when you mentor someone, you find that there are more efficient methods to accomplish what you do.

Here is a case in point. I was stationed at Fort Leonard Wood, Missouri, as the senior program analyst for a one-star command and a one-man band. I was in the middle of making doctrine, fielding equipment, and evaluating an exercise in Korea when my mother passed away. I went on emergency leave and spent an entire day downloading information about every effort I was working on. I had an extensive contact list as well as reams of paper in three-ring binders for each effort. I did what I could in a short time and went on leave.

When I came back, nothing new was in my binders, but I found the documents were now on the shared drive along with notes and the contact list with meeting dates and times. I was amazed at what the section had done for me. My section kept my programs afloat in my absence, and I was truly thankful. From that day on, when I returned to the office, I made sure I had another person who was just as familiar with my programs as I was. In fact, I started calling them "our programs."

Sharing work documents, analysis, and some decisions with coworkers and keeping them in the loop will pay huge dividends when you must leave in a hurry.

44

No Is Not an Option

Say no by saying yes.

As leaders, we hate to hear the word "no" when we want to do something. As a junior enlisted soldier when I was young, I witnessed quite a lot of senior people tell the commander that they couldn't do something. It never works out in the person's favor when they say no to a commander without a very through explanation. Having a well thought-out explanation after "no" is the key—and may even save a career. When a staff member understands the intent of what a commander is trying to do, the staff member needs to look at all the ways to go around obstacles while meeting or exceeding the provided intent.

As leaders, we always have one or more people we report and provide results to. This is all in a day's work. Being tactful when you want to say no takes guts as well. When I was asked my opinion and did not agree with the presented path, I made sure I had a detailed analysis along with projected results prepared.

Instead of saying no, I usually said something like this: "Sir/ Ma'am, I don't 100 percent agree with the projected path. However, this section has [or I have] developed another course of action that we [or I] believe will reach the end state with minimal risk." After saying this to a general officer, I needed to make sure I had my analysis on hand and ready to be briefed. I had said no without saying no and offered what I saw as a better alternative.

So if you're the leader receiving the brief, don't get offended if someone says they can't do something. Now is the time to reflect on past leadership principles—to ask important questions and request the data that might change your mind.

Whether saying no to someone or being told no, use the situation as an opportunity to show your expertise—but always be prepared to hear that no matter how good your analysis was, they are still going to use the other plan.

Remember, when you understand the boss's intent, saying an absolute no is never a good idea. It is always preferable to turn "I can't do that" into "here's what I can do"—offer a better course of action that is legal, ethical, feasible, cost-effective, and sensible, with the least amount of risk.

Dr. Mark P. Michels, LTC, USA (ret)

45

Here's to Your Health

Healthy body, healthy mind.

Despite advertisements for diet pills and workout videos, our American society is overweight, to an extent that varies by region and how studies measure obesity. It's no secret that having a healthy body will result in fewer doctor appointments and taking fewer medications. Your time away from work may be reduced, and you may be more productive. Of course, accidents happen; people break bones. And while genetics plays a vital role in your health, don't let heredity stop you from becoming healthy.

For most of my career, I was a lean, mean fighting machine … then I got a desk job and injured my knee, requiring reconstructive surgery. Being in a cast from the top of my ankle to my groin made any movement a huge task. I went on like this for many months and developed a blood clot just above my knee, which required me to stay still and mostly bedridden for two to three weeks. This happened when I was in my early to mid thirties, and I gained some significant weight that I found really hard to lose.

In my younger days when I gained a little weight, I would just run longer distances and spend more time in the gym, but working long hours and sitting behind a desk made maintaining regulation weight a chore. Following a ten-year gap after earning my bachelor's degree, I started a master's online, which required even more seat time in front of a computer after work. My cognitive functions have always been the same when it comes to work processes and mental discipline, but as I got older, I always worried about dropping weight before a physical fitness test. I noticed that it took me longer to get the extra weight off and to develop the motivation to try new things and be more adventurous.

To combat weight gain, I spent all my time, hours and hours, in the gym between work and school. Higher-level education and being fit were and are essential for advancing in the military, but unfortunately this left little time with my wife and kids. As you can imagine, my family life suffered, and I knew I had to change—it was imperative to make time for my family. Once I developed a good rhythm among work, school, and the gym, I was able to make plans with my wife and kids, and I felt better both mentally and physically.

In my opinion, there is very little separation between having a healthy body and a healthy mind: both are important to achieve and maintain.

46

True Friendship

True friends will be there for you through thick and thin.

This principle may not seem like the usual leadership Lesson Learned I talk about, but the reliance on a true friend is important to any leader, no matter what level you're at on the corporate or military ladder. Having someone to call in the middle of the night to discuss work, relationships, or situational issues is valuable for all leaders. Sometimes, having someone you trust to provide a true and unbiased opinion is a great way for a leader to get a commonsense check for simple to complex problems. A true friend can be a high school or college buddy, or someone you spent time with while in the service.

No matter where you find your true friends, they should have these characteristics.

- They have their own opinions that do not always mirror yours.
- They go straight to "How can I help?" before requiring background information when you bring up a problem.
- No matter how long it has been since your last communication, they will always be able to talk with you as if the last time the two of you spoke was just yesterday.

- They won't be able to help you when you do something really stupid, because they will be sitting next to you on the jail bench.

These are not hard and fast rules but represent what a true friend is to me. These characteristics are worth seeking out and have served me well for a long time.

To this day, I value this type of friendship and work hard to maintain it—because the other side of having a true friend is reciprocating the effort. Life happens and people change, but true friendship will endure.

47

Be a Good Sport

Always have good sportsmanship.

Nobody likes to lose at anything—unless it's shedding off unwanted fat. But most people like being right and being a winner. When I was in school, and continuing after high school, I played sports and participated in various competitions. Usually when you get many type A personalities in one location and tell them to go play, we don't hear "Go play," we hear "Go to battle and don't return until it is won!"

But whether the "battle" is salesman of the month or a post-wide basketball tournament, be a good sport and encourage good sportsmanship. When we see actions unbecoming of professional competition, we need to discipline accordingly. If for some reason you forget who and where you are as a leader and demonstrate poor sportsmanship, your supervisors, peers, and subordinates will see it, and inevitably you will lose respect. Lose gracefully, with congratulations to the winner and a handshake.

Healthy competition within the workspace can be a team-building experience and a proving ground for potential leaders. Show good sportsmanship, and remember: if you lost, practice, practice, and practice more so that next time you will win. And if you and your team did win, be good sports and don't gloat. A little trash-talking is acceptable in some places but not all, so be aware of your environment and act like the professional you are.

48

No Regrets

Don't go through life saying "shoulda, woulda, coulda."

This is not just a leadership lesson, it's a life lesson. Have you ever been presented with an opportunity that came out of nowhere and with some contemplation might be feasible? I think everyone has at some point in life. My advice is don't live your life with regrets.

I'm not saying quit your job or business and cash in your IRA and 401(k) and travel the world on a backpacking trip, but if you are in a place in your life where you can make some changes without sacrificing lots of money or your real property, go for it. I can't tell you how many people I meet in my military and civilian travels who tell me that getting out of the military was a big mistake and that they would have been able to retire already had they remained.

Do yourself a favor, and save yourself some sleepless nights: when opportunity knocks, sit down and rationally determine whether making a change is feasible, sensible, and cost-effective. Allow your significant other to help in the planning. Who knows, they might be more excited about the opportunity than you are and may see more advantages to the change than you had previously considered.

Also seek out others who made the change and see how they did it. Ask about the challenges and how they overcame them. Seeking out meaningful mentorship always should be encouraged.

If you decide to go for an opportunity, don't look back. If the path leads you somewhere you didn't want to go, start over and seek out other opportunities. Just be thoughtful, diligent, and resourceful in your planning. And always have a plan B on the back burner. Don't go through life saying, "I should have," "I could have," or "I would have."

49

Be Ready to Adjust

Know when to "cut sling load"—or better yet, when and how to adjust efforts.

"Sling load" refers to the hanging cargo attached to a helicopter, which in some dangerous circumstances might have to be let go to save the aircraft from destruction or damage. "Cut sling load" is a military saying conveyed with a hand and arm signal, used when a situation is going south and the leader of the mission or task has decided to stop and try something else. As leaders, when do we know to "cut sling load"? Do we wait days, hour, or minutes to see if something changes? How do we know when enough is enough? The answer may seem simple at first, but I assure you the decision to stop all efforts is huge and may have repercussions.

The ability to avoid issuing a "cut sling load" command begins with the first planning meeting. During planning, the staff should always conduct a risk assessment for the most dangerous or most likely to happen scenarios during a mission. Each planned risk mitigation measure contains the start of a contingency, "plan B," a modification to the plan, or at the very least, a decision point that needs to be war-gamed and documented.

When faced with a decision point, in fact no leader should ever say "cut sling load"—they should say "start XYZ plan" so that everyone knows and understands what to do. If you hear a leader say "cut sling load" or something similar in meaning, you know the planning staff failed to identify risks and prepare acceptable, suitable, distinguishable, and complete alternate plans.

Deal with Your Problems

It is OK to have problems, but it is not OK to allow them to continue.

Everyone at some point in life has had small or large problems. There are many psychological reasons that people thrive on conflict or continue to repeat the same mistakes. But mental illness aside, problems need to be dealt with quickly. As I said early in this book (principle 4), not every problem merits emergency status, but something must be done.

Having an extensive business background is **a** great thing that taught me to conduct a root cause analysis. This is a fundamental tool to help define and construct solutions to problems. A root cause analysis is an illustration of cause and effect that resulted in the problem, with branches of causal relationships. Once you determine the roots causes, or causes, of a problem, you must determine which elements are under your control and which are not.

When I have demonstrated a root cause analysis to clients, it has been an eye-opener. I have found solutions for customers that were as simple as hiring another person or that pinpointed the supervisor's lack of decision-making and sticking to the decision. Whichever method you choose to define a problem, determining mitigation measures is totally up to you. Whichever method you choose—such as a root cause analysis, a decision matrix, or focused brainstorming— don't let problems define who you are. Deal with them, and quickly.

Afterword

Don't ever forget those who have helped you along life's journey.

Throughout my thirty-year career in the Army, I have helped people get to where they thought was the best place for them to be. Conversely, people have helped me to become successful in my career.

Thinking about the past, with surprising clarity I can recall each person by their full name and how they helped me. The people who have helped me include drill sergeants, supervisors, peers, friends, family members, complete strangers—and I'm sure God played a part in my life every day. Whether someone helped you knowingly or not, their help has been valuable to you. If you recognize that someone's decision helped you without their knowing it, go out of your way to thank them. They might be surprised to find that their actions had a positive outcome for someone, and they might continue their efforts or be inspired to offer more assistance.

I pride myself on being an independent person who rarely requires help. So when I'm at my wits' end and feel I have exhausted all avenues to help myself, then you can rest assured a big problem exists. Any way that one or more people can offer advice or additional resources to help my situation is appreciated. It has always seemed that when I thought I was at the bottom, I somehow got rescued.

I have found that there are a few ways to thank people for their help and demonstrate thankfulness. Most people just want acknowledgment that the act or advice they gave you has been appreciated, so a simple thank-you would suffice.

As I write, it was just last week that I was on my way to go hunting and found an SUV in a ditch on a steep and muddy road. I stopped and asked the two young women if they were all right and needed help. The driver said that she got a phone call, and when she had pulled over to the side of the road to answer it, the truck just slid into the ditch.

The first thing that came to my mind was that she had done the right thing by not talking on the phone while driving, and she wasn't playing around. She also said that everyone with the means to pull her out was at work and couldn't help.

I got back in my truck and slowly pulled up to her rear bumper, then attached a tow strap to her tow hitch and to my front tow hook. I put the truck in four low and just idled her vehicle back onto the road. Then I unhooked the strap, put everything back, and made sure the vehicle was still good to be on the road. The young ladies tried to give me some money, but I refused. I told them that if my kids were in need someday, I would hope someone would stop and help them without requiring anything in return. They were truly thankful, and I said that if they found someone in need and they had the means to help, they should not hesitate. No good deed goes unnoticed, and it may open up an opportunity for you to "pay it forward."

Throughout my career, when I've run into soldiers I recruited or soldiers I served with, they have all told me of their good memories and have shared some examples of how I had a positive influence in their life. Although I had only a short time serving as a drill sergeant, I've encountered two soldiers I pushed through training, and their comments were along the lines of "firm but fair."

Interactions like these are far and few between but all the more inspiring. I'm glad I had a positive influence, and I didn't even know it. A simple thank-you should be all that is required. We're all in this together, so don't underestimate your own ability to help people every day.

About the Author

Dr. Mark Michels served in the US Army for over thirty years, retiring from active duty in October 2019 with the rank of Lieutenant Colonel. He enlisted in the infantry in 1988 as a private and after twelve years of service accepted a full Green to Gold Scholarship to the ROTC program of Syracuse University. Through his varied career he achieved the rank of Sergeant First Class (E-7) and in May 2001 was commissioned a Second Lieutenant as an Air Defense Artilleryman, later transitioning to the Nuclear Nonproliferation Officer (FA-52) functional area. He has deployed to the Middle East and Africa in various campaigns and missions.

Dr. Michels has earned an associate's degree from Mohawk Valley Community College, a bachelor's from SUNY Poly Technical Institute, a master's from American Military University, a graduate certificate from Post University, and a doctorate from Northcentral University. Dr. Michels is married to Gabrielle, with whom he has four children, Tanner, Mason, Hunter, and Haley. He resides in upstate New York.